52
Gifts

from me
to you

NORTH LIGHT BOOKS

CINCINNATI, OHIO

To ....

From ....

Date ....

1

My favorite
memory of
you is...

2 You're beautiful when...

3 You're special because...

4

You inspire
me by...

5 I always appreciate
the way you...

1 ....
....
....

2 ....
....
....

3 ....
....
....

4 ....
....
....

5 ....
....
....

6

An important
moment for
us was...

7 Our path
has been...

8 The world is a better
place because you...

9 You taught me to care about...

10 I'm so glad you...

11 You have changed my life by...

12

I've always wanted
to ask you...

13   I've always wanted to tell you...

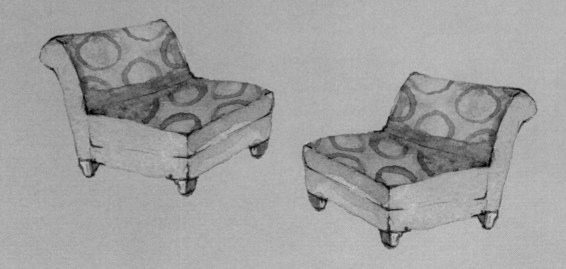

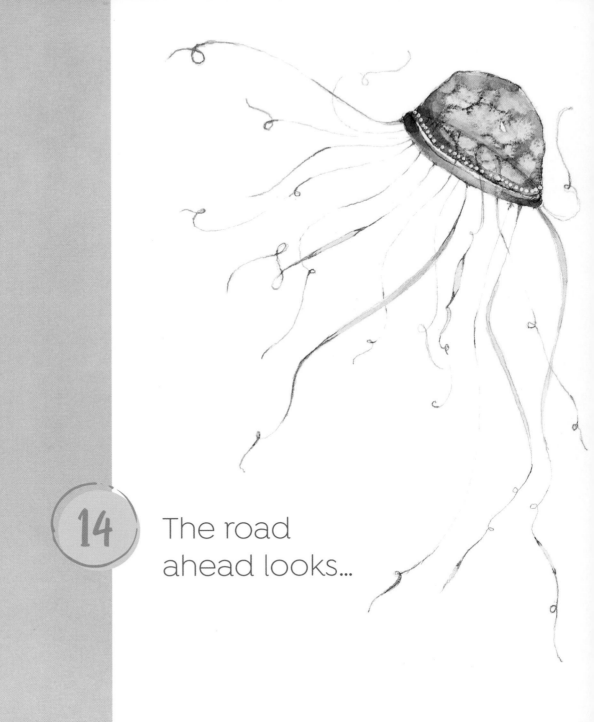

14 The road
ahead looks...

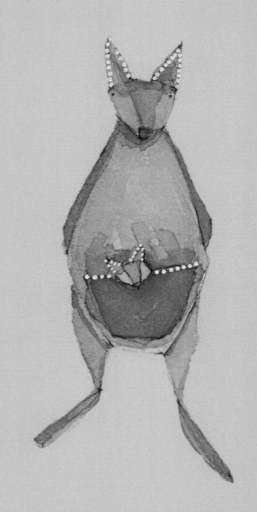

15 I remember the
first time we...

16 You inspire me to...

17 You brighten
my world by...

18

My life is better
because you...

19 Our relationship is...

1 ....

....

....

2 ....

....

....

3 ....

....

....

4 ....

....

....

5 ....

....

....

 I'm grateful for you because...

 21 You make
me feel
better when...

22   I remember when we
faced the challenge of...

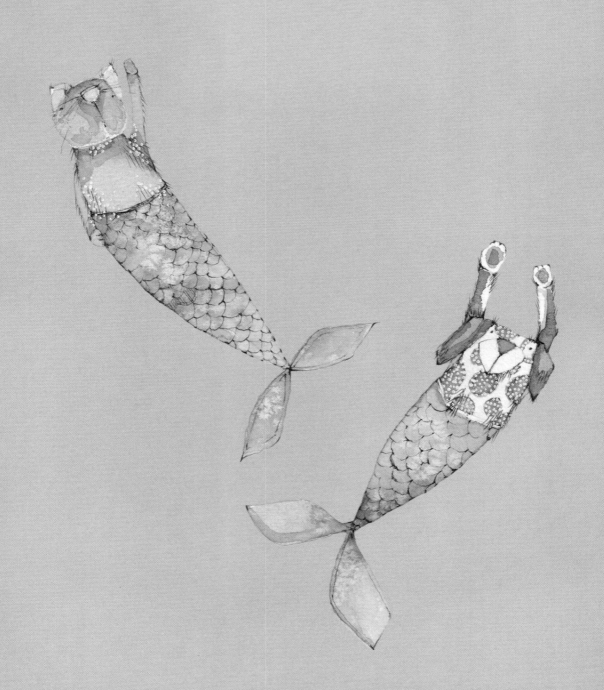

23 We're so different because...

....

....

....

....

....

....

....

....

....

....

....

....

....

....

....

24   I treasure...

25 I love our inside joke...

26 It's the little things that matter like...

27 Five things I love
about you...

1 ....

....

....

2 ....

....

....

3 ....

....

....

4 ....

....

....

5 ....

....

....

 **28** You make me feel...

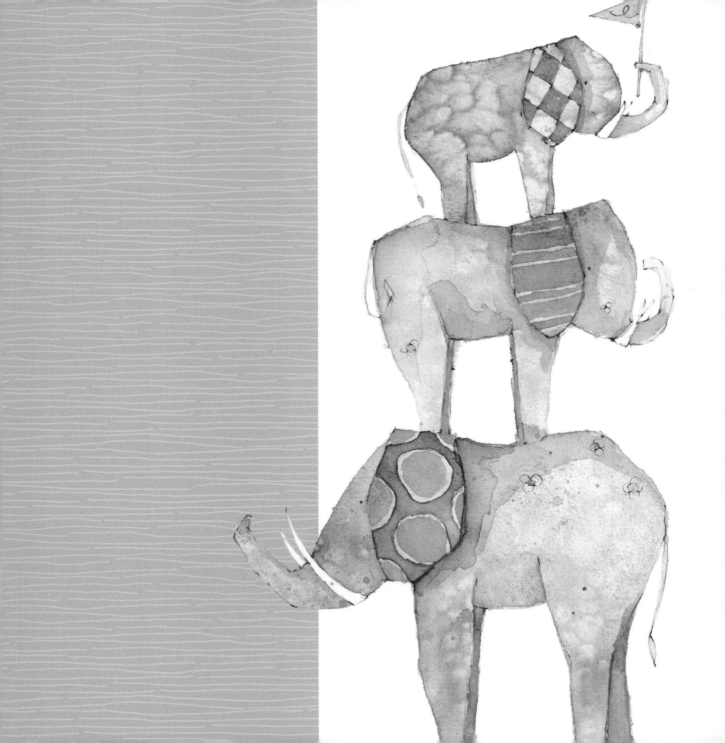

29 You've shown me strength by...

....

....

....

....

....

....

....

....

....

....

....

....

....

....

30 We're so alike
because...

31 A quote that reminds me of you is...

32

You helped
me discover
the magic of...

(33) You helped me to overcome...

34 You've taught me...

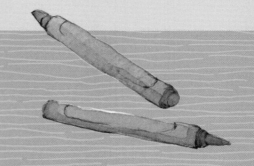

1 ....
....
....

2 ....
....
....

3 ....
....
....

4 ....
....
....

5 ....
....
....

35 *I hope you...*

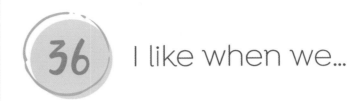

36 I like when we...

37   I love that you care about...

38

I love that we can
laugh about...

39 You showed me the value of...

....
....
....
....
....
....
....
....
....
....
....
....
....
....
....

40 You lifted me up when...

 You've made me stronger by...

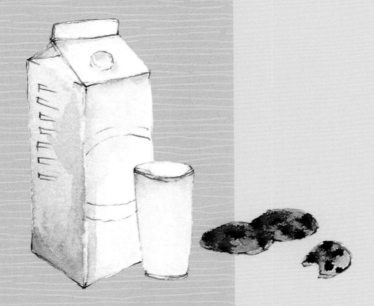

42 You show me love by...

 **43** You taught me about forgiveness when...

 **44** You helped me when...

45

Never forget that...

46 I feel connected to you when...

47

An adventure
we had...

 **48** When I look back on...

49   I wish that we could...

I remember the good
times when we...

1 ....

....

....

2 ....

....

....

3 ....

....

....

4 ....

....

....

5 ....

....

....

My hope for us is...

You taught me to dream when...

ABOUT THE ARTIST

Artist Danielle Donaldson has walked a creative path for as long as she can remember. Her love of art began, as with most young souls, with a big box of crayons and a stack of coloring books. Over time, she focused her artistic efforts on watercolor and graphite drawing techniques, and eventually received her degree in graphic design. Her love of fine art paired with her skills as a graphic designer have provided her with an uncommon partnership of intuition and practicality. Her use of big color palettes and delicately drawn details allows her to spin the ordinary into imaginative, well-balanced compositions. She continues to grow as an artist by fully embracing the creative process in all she does and with each story she tells. She thoroughly enjoys sharing her process and imagination through online classes, in-person workshops, social media and in her books, *creativeGIRL: Mixed Media Techniques for an Artful Life* and *The Art of Creative Watercolor: Inspiration and Techniques for Imaginative Drawing and Painting*. Visit Danielle's website, DanielleDonaldson.com.

a content + ecommerce company

Other fine North Light Books are available from your favorite
bookstore, art supply store or online supplier. Visit our website at fwmedia.com.

23 22 21 20 19   5 4 3 2 1

DISTRIBUTED IN THE U.K. AND EUROPE
BY F&W MEDIA INTERNATIONAL LTD
Pynes Hill Court, Pynes Hill, Rydon Lane,
Exeter, EX2 5AZ, United Kingdom
Tel: (+44) 1392 797680
Email: enquiries@fwmedia.com

ISBN 13: 978-1-4403-0101-8

Edited by Amy Jones
Artwork by Danielle Donaldson
Designed by Clare Finney
Production Managed by Debbie Thomas